LOVE ME
meditations

There exists already, a version of ourselves who has
already become everything we ever dreamed of,
if only we can get out of our own way and allow
ourselves to actually believe it, feel it, and be it.

LOVE ME
meditations

CULTIVATING WHOLENESS OF BEING

T.M. CAMPBELL

ROBERT T. NORTON

Library and Archives Canada Cataloguing in Publication
Campbell, Tricia M., 1970 –
Norton, Robert, 1963 –

Love Me Meditations /
T. M. Campbell & Robert T. Norton

Paperback ISBN 978-1-7387333-2-3

First paperback edition March 2023

Cover Design by
T.M. Campbell & Jasmine K. Sikand

Published by INVIBE
www.thisistrishcampbell.com/publications

For *YOU,* who embodies the courage to journey inward; to drop from the mind into the heart, and live this precious life from the inside out.

"The privilege of a lifetime is being who you are."

- Joseph Campbell

CONTENTS

"You and I are all as much continuous with the physical Universe as a wave is continuous with the ocean."

– Alan Watts

INTRODUCTION
by T. M. CAMPBELL

*L*ove Me Meditations is an extension of author T.M. Campbell's *LOVE ME: Awakening to Healing, Self-Love and Liberation.*

That which comes from within us, ripples out into the world around us. What we came here to experience in our human form is ultimately the manifestation of the Soul's journey.

We come into our physical bodies at birth knowing exactly who we are and why we came here, or rather, our Souls do. Our Soul knows we came here to love, to create, to evolve and to reach our potential as human beings – in every which way. Because of societal influences, we soon forget that assignment, mostly because our early childhood development is centered around teaching us to participate in society, rather than remember our *Divinity*. Hence why later on, in our fully-developed adult years, we may feel our lives lack a sense of meaning and purpose.

Often we seek meaning because we have disconnected from the wisdom of our Soul and our natural way of being. We live inside the stories we tell ourselves that make us feel better about not being in alignment with our Soul. That disconnection partially stems from our conditioning, in addition to the trauma and wounds we experience beginning early on in life – from the womb, throughout our childhood and into adulthood.

We might attempt to convince ourselves we are okay and can navigate life just fine, yet the energy of those wounds – the feelings and emotions of them – remains in our body somewhere. The energy of our stored emotions becomes stagnant, even malignant, if we don't actively process and release that energy. Those old wounds eventually become our foundation of operating our lives, and our relationships suffer. We suffer.

Awakening is the remembering of the *who, what and why.* Through our process of awakening, we begin to connect the dots of our past experiences to our present reality. We begin to heal.

Healing is at the root of our journey through this human experience, ultimately remembering who we are, to embody a greater knowing, find love for ourselves, and realize our ultimate potential.

In *LOVE ME*, I shared my journey of healing and awakening to a truth that I didn't know who I was anymore. I had abandonned my true self. Over time, I had subconsciously created a *"somebody"* in order to fit in; in order to be accepted, seen, heard, and loved. Yet that "acceptance" and "feeling seen and heard" felt empty, because that *"somebody"* wasn't me.

I could seldom *feel loved enough* because I didn't have a true relationship with myself. I was operating – though not aware at that time – on the basis of how others received, accepted, and loved me. I shifted how I showed up, shaving off pieces of myself. Over time, I had become a fraction of my true self; increasingly fragmented in order to feel that love and acceptance, and further detached from my wholeness of being.

This overarching energy of subconsciously shifting who we are at our core, at the Soul level, can manifest in infinite ways; it is different for each of us. This is why I have shared my story. When we share our stories, we heal, but there is also healing for those with whom we share our stories. My story is my story, and your story is yours, but there are parallels that can be drawn from all of our stories into the lives of many.

We don't have to be defined externally, or by the stories of our past. We came here to create Heaven on Earth; to experience the beauty of our inherent *Divinity*, the depth of human connection and a profound unconditional love that burns eternal in our Soul's core. This occurs naturally through the empowered creation that's driven from our Soul.

Robert and I wrote these meditation prompts with the knowing that unconditional love for ourselves, our healing and our human experience deepens when we allow ourselves to drop out of the mind and into the heart.

If you have read *LOVE ME*, these meditations will feel familiar to you. These prompts are an extension of the lessons and wisdoms I shared in the book. Through reading, we can gain an understanding in our minds. We learn and glean wisdoms; perhaps even have an *a-ha* moment.

That said, as much as we have the tendency to try to figure it all out in our heads, healing doesn't only happen in the mind. Our emotional healing happens through the body, through feeling and being at the intersection of the heart and Soul. That's where the magic unfolds. Allowing the feelings to rise to the surface, processing them and then applying the learnings that enter, we become aware; we feel; we understand; and then we act on and apply the lessons in our lives. Through this integration, real change occurs.

This book is a tool to assist us in transmuting those feelings and emotions, whatever they might be – pain, anger, sadness, love, joy – bubbling within us into profound transformation, through gleaning the wisdoms they hold. And so this book is a bridge from our societal programming to stepping into all that we came here to be.

There are no "rules" with these meditation prompts. They're grouped in overarching themes, however, you can use and apply them as you wish. Additionally, here are some ways you might experiment with them:

- As a daily practice – Select one a day, in chronological order, or select a theme to begin with, according to the area of yourself where you seek greater understanding.

- As an oracle – Come here each day and let yourself be guided to whatever page the book opens to. This is the Universe, your Spirit guides, or perhaps your higher self speaking to you.

- When you are having an "off" day.

- When you are feeling high on life!

- When you feel a need to drop into your heart.

- Whichever manner *feels good* for you in a given moment.

- You can combine any of the above or create your own process.

Whichever way you use them, allow yourself to be guided from your heart and intuition, rather than your mind. Remember there is no endpoint. This is about the journey. And, the deeper it gets, the deeper it gets!

The Universe is always supporting us in allowing our Soul's journey to unfold. It may not always make sense to us, and it doesn't have to! We can rest assured we are always Universally supported and we are always carried where we are meant to be at any given moment along our journey.

Trust the process!
in peace + love,

T. M. Campbell

"Each one of us has to be our true self:
Fresh, solid, at ease, loving, and compassionate.
When we are our true selves, not only do we benefit,
But everyone around us profits from our presence."

— Thich Nhat Hanh

INTRODUCTION
by ROBERT T. NORTON

*L*et's start with a radical thought: what if there was no right way and no wrong way to use these meditations? How liberating would that be for you? How uncomfortable would that be for you? In answering each of these questions, and ultimately of how you may choose to approach these meditations, it is useful to go deeper and ask yourself: *Why, Why Not* and *What if?*

The *Why,* the *Why Not,* and the *What If* is where it gets personal. It is the freedom you give yourself to experiment and to push the boundaries; and that freedom is where you will meet your expansion. How far are you willing to go? The answer is different for each of us. The key is to recognize and give yourself that freedom and to push, at your own pace, beyond your comfort zone.

That is precisely what happened for me, after I read *LOVE ME.* I was so inspired by what I had read, and much of it resonated so strongly with me that I had a *What If* moment. It struck me that a book of meditations based on *LOVE ME* was the perfect way to highlight the wisdoms in that book in a very practical and accessible way; *What If,* indeed?

Love Me Meditations is a work of expansion. Trish and I took our respective experiences with *LOVE ME*, and asked the question of *Why Not?* Our answer was to experiment, to push our boundaries, and to collaborate to find this next destination on our individual journeys.

Let's get back to your journey! These meditation prompts are meant to provoke reflective thought about you, and in particular about your life experience. The answers, and specifically the emotions and ideas that they produce are uniquely yours. And that is the primary reason why the binary concept of right way and wrong way do not apply.

Do you live in a very goal-oriented, productivity-output-measuring society? Why do we gravitate towards keeping score? Why not challenge yourself to abandon that frame of reference and instead embrace the meditations tabula rasa? A healthier and a deliberate choice, is to practice these meditations for the experience of them; in a spirit of openness and curiosity as to where they might lead you. *Why Not* take that journey? Take what you need from them in the moment, and leave the rest… for now, with the awareness that in your future, you may need some of that rest at various points along your path.

What If you find pleasure and satisfaction in the discoveries of your Self that these meditations may lead you to? Strive to open yourself to these discoveries; avoid passing judgement and holding rigid expectations attached to desired outcomes. Instead, marvel at the gift of your multifaceted complexity and the rich subtleties that are uniquely you. Employ these meditations as a conduit, a way to focus your energies and emotions into the most supremely important relationship in your life… *YOU*!

Let the meditations point out the roadblocks and potholes that societal programing has cunningly applied to you over the decades. It is these roadblocks that dim your Soul light, and keep you distanced from a pure relationship with your Self. A regular practice with these meditations may enable you to navigate around the roadblocks and potholes, towards your true Self and its expansion.

How you choose to use this book is up to you! Perhaps you will pick a meditation at a regular interval, or at a random moment as you feel the need. Will you choose to journal your thoughts and feelings that arise from your reflection on that meditation? Maybe you will opt to explore a meditation in conversation with a close friend, or with a trusted group of like-minded souls. Why not consider dabbling in each of them at a point in time? It is worth considering that varying your approach occasionally can only serve to enrich your experience and broaden your expansion.

Resist a purely linear application of these meditations attached to a specific outcome. Instead, embrace them with a spirit of *What If*: curiosity, possibility, and creativity. Let the meditations guide you into your expansion, towards a deeper relationship with your Self, and into a more profound connection with your Soul light.

Consider your awareness on the *Language* of your thoughts that arise from a meditation. *Could* language opens you to infinite possibilities; it is the language of discovery and curiosity. Conversely, *Should* and *Must* language leads you into obligations, and it is the language of anxiety, resentment, and stagnation.

How are you responding to both the meditations and to your *Language*? Are you reflexively passing judgements, or are you asking questions? Are you asking the right questions? Questions from your heart, asked with a spirit of curiosity and of seeking, are what can lead you to a new path of expansion which has been waiting patiently for you.

Circling back to the opening radical thought: what if there was no *right way* and no *wrong way* to use these meditations? What if you used these meditations in the spirit of imperfect action? That would mean releasing yourself from the deeply-flawed societal paradigm of perfection, and from there, exploring imperfect action; how it *Could* become the scaffolding of your expansion. *Could* you seek comfort in your discomfort? *Could* you throw away the *Easy Button* for this aspect of your journey, and perhaps for other aspects of your life as well? Show up and challenge yourself, always!

Namaste!

RTN

I

BEING

∞

HONOURING OUR TRUTH

–

Honouring our Truth is about honouring
all that we are; all that drives and empowers us;
cultivating love and compassion for ourselves as
we meet the hard things head on, rather than resist.

We live from our Truth – and our life truly becomes
our own – when we stop abandoning ourselves
in order to meet other people's expectations for it;
when we shine rather than hide our *Divine Light*;

In honouring our Truth, in trust, we become
more empowered, more whole in our being,
and we allow our Soul the journey that
it came here to take, to heal and evolve.

WE ALREADY ARE

—

There is no becoming;
we already are…
we have always been.

One hand stretched behind us,
in the process of letting go.
One hand extended in front of us,
reaching to touch the edge of the unknown.

SOUL SPEAKS

—

There is always a spark inside of us...
a quiet voice within
waiting to be seen and heard.

Soul speaks,
but are we listening?
Are we tuning in?

Allow yourself a moment to be in stillness.
What do you hear when you tune in?

TRUE SELF

—

It is courageous, brave, even revolutionary
to show up as your true self.

Especially when the world is constantly
trying to make you someone else.

Once we can see behind all the external noise,
once we dare to journey within,
we will know the *Truth* of who we are.

WE ARE OUR OWN HERO

—

Role playing airbrushes who we truly are at our core.
Our innate Self is suppressed, and this is
a quiet act of violence against ourselves.

It is the unique facets of our inner-being
that fuel our inner light of self-expression.
The light that, over time, we have been taught to dim
in exchange for acceptance and a sense of belonging.

Ultimately your light is your *Hero.*
Embrace your *Hero* on a regular basis.

FIND YOUR PEOPLE

—

Find your people.
As much as we try to convince ourselves
that we can go it alone…
nothing of significance is
achieved independently.
We need each other.

As you travel your unique path,
give yourself permission to
outgrow people, places and things.

Let go of anyone that requires
you to convince them of your worthiness.

Surround yourself with people
who see your light already, and who are
in alignment with where you aspire to go.

WORTHINESS

—

We are all worthy from birth…
of love, of acceptance, and
of realizing our greatest potential.

Worthiness is our birthright.

There is nothing to prove in order to
receive all that is waiting for us:
abundance, freedom, creativity, success,
love, peace... however that looks for us.

If there is a dream or a spark of desire
in our heart, it means it is possible;
otherwise, our Soul would not speak it.

Now the question is, are we listening?

BUILDING A HOME

—

Building a *Home* inside of ourselves,
is the ultimate act of self-love.
Within this *Home* we find both
our liberation and our salvation.

Building our own inner strength, this *Home*,
this connection to our core being, enables us
to embody resilience in the face of life's challenges.

Our *Home* also allows us to be there
for each other in a more compassionate way.

Building a *Home* inside means
that no matter where we are,
we are always *Home*.

THE GIFT OF BEING

—

Giving myself the gift of being.
What more could I need?
What more could I want?

It has been so long since the last time.
A day free from manufactured
obligations and societal noise.

Today, there will be no
shoulds, musts, or *need-to's*.

Today, there will only be
the soft whispers of a Muse...
leading me into my expansion.

NATURE

—

Nature constantly reminds us who we are.

We are connected to all that is around us.
Natural intelligence communicates with us:
the wind whispers in the forest
and the trees sing in reply;
the rhythm of the waves
replicates our breath, in and out;
the sun and the moon share their energies
and infinite wisdom with us
in constant transmission.

And we remember.

GRATITUDE

—

Gratitude is a practice.
It fortifies the foundation of our being.

Gratitude invites us to take our well-being into our own hands.
It allows our current reality to be enough.

Gratitude connects us to the present moment.
It is a tool we can access at any time.

Gratitude is the portal to our higher self.
It delivers us to our spiritual integrity.

Gratitude is our light through any darkness.
It reminds us *we are enough* already.

What are you grateful for today?

COMPLETE

—

I am full
and complete,
yet infinite.

And so,
I am
to be continued…

THE BALANCE OF
GIVING AND RECEIVING

—

Giving and receiving is a concept
that seems quite simple.
Yet when the integral give and take
is imbalanced, frustration is inevitable.

Frustration always has a tipping point.
Keeping score holds the energy of lack;
the energy of "not-enough."

Embodying the energy of abundance,
we know there is always enough;
that there is a Universal, karmic balance…
and there is no need for keeping score.

NATURAL INTELLIGENCE

—

Be guided by the natural intelligence of
your heart, versus your ego's demands for comfort.

The natural intelligence that flows
through all things is present and open,
without resistance or unnecessary interference.

As humans, we easily can get in our own way,
and we can often get in each other's way.
That is our ego calling the shots,
always demanding its comfort.

It is our heart that is the true essence of who we are,
and that enables us to reach and be in our
highest and most authentic expression of Self.
This is where the *Magic* resides!

AUTHENTICITY

—

Stepping into our authenticity,
into the truest expression
of who we came here to be.

It is not a license to be reckless
with our ego, or with other
people's feelings or emotions.

It is a balance of being true to Self,
practicing self-awareness,
minding ego's presence,
and applying healthy boundaries.

All of these practices allow
us to be heart-centred and present
in our relationships…
to see and be seen;
to hear and be heard;
to love and be loved.

II

MYTHS

PERFECTION

—

Perfection is a myth.
It is not attainable.

We are not beings of perfection…
rather, we are beings of expansion.

What if we were to dismantle
the myth of perfection,
by embracing and expanding
our imperfect humanity?

FAILURE

–

Failure is not something that
we should avoid; rather, it is
something that we may embrace
to explore the lessons it offers.

Failure is essential to our success.
It is inevitable and integral
to deepening our wisdom;
and is a companion of true learning.

Become open to getting it wrong.
Recognize that we can't possibly
know all of the answers.
Understand and accept that we
can learn something from *everyone*.

Set your intention to being open to failure
and allow space for learning within that.

INVISIBILITY

–

Might invisibility, or dimming be a shield that I
deploy to protect myself from rejection?

At an early age, we begin to learn the parts
of ourselves that we can feel safe expressing,
and those parts that we need to keep hidden
to fit in, to be received and accepted by others.

Ask yourself, *"What is serving me*
by becoming invisible or dimming my light?
"What is my soul's desire for me?"
"Is my soul's desire simply to be who I am,
with no need to convince
anyone else of my worthiness?"

There really is no need for
protecting myself from rejection
when I am in integrity with my soul.

EXPECTATIONS

—

Over the course of our life's journey –
our Soul's journey – so many of our
experiences and outcomes are
influenced and even determined by the
expectations of others and societal agreements.

When we go along with these expectations
we can end up depleted, frustrated and miserable;
our life can lack meaning and purpose.
The same feelings may arise when we place our
expectations upon other people.

Can you relate?

FEELING FEAR

—

Fear is only a feeling.
Feelings are temporary.

Either we manage fear…
or it manages us.

Fear is ultimately about
our ego's need to control.

Fear is driven by the ego.
Courage is cultivated in the Soul.

PERFECTLY IMPERFECT

—

The truth is hard to hear, see, feel and face at times,
and that is because it reveals our denial of reality.

Ultimately, what we are doing is pretending that
we are not imperfect, and doing our best to
convince everyone of that, including ourselves.

We have been taught that if we are feeling off,
then there is something wrong with us, and
that imperfection is to be avoided at all costs.

Perfection is a myth; a societal control mechanism.

Let us not seek outcomes of perfection...
Instead, we could find liberation in our imperfection, for
it is both the foundation and scaffolding of our humanity.

INTRINSIC BEING

—

How much time and energy do we spend
proving our worth in this materialistic system?

We are programed to accept that our
personal value should be measured by:
possessions, job titles, and productivity
over our presence of being; over
our connection to our own Divinity.

Operating within a frame of materialistic values,
we uphold a system that creates and thrives off
of our insecurity and imperfect humanity.

What if we chose to be who we naturally are
without needing to prove anything?
Without seeking external validation?

Communing with our intuition, connecting with
our deep inner-knowing as our compass;
and aligning with our intrinsic being.

DEPROGRAMMING

—

We came into this life, full of promise, hope and
undeniable being… simply being who we are naturally,
with a deep inner knowing of our of true potential.

Decades of societal programming mould and shape us.
Consequently, we become adept at shifting ourselves
to accommodate how others prefer to receive us,
and these accomodations carry significant costs.

When we accomodate the energy of certain situations,
We are not radiating our authentic *Divine Light*.

In shining our inherent, natural light
by being in our authentic expression,
we reclaim the power of writing our own story.

EASY BUTTON

–

There is no *Easy Button* for healing.

We can avoid our pain and grief –
temporarily – but it will show up again,
in other people, places and things.

If we attempt to hit the *Easy Button*,
we may miss the opportunity
that gifts us our transformation.

Our pain holds wisdom.
Our emotions hold information.
Each time we choose to move through –
not around – our pain and our emotions,
we open ourselves to higher levels of consciousness.

ASSUMPTION & JUDGEMENT

–

Let's not judge each other for stepping outside the box.
After all, we were never meant to be beings of perfection.

Often, we judge in others what we subconsciously
believe to be our own shortcoming(s).
But our "shortcomings," what we might view
as our faults, or imperfections, are part of our humanity.

Assumption is the close companion of *Judgement.*
When one appears, the other is certain to follow in haste.
Two sides of the same coin – the currency of Ego
– that can only purchase envy, jealousy. and misery.

We can move away from *Judgement & Assumption* by
embracing our imperfection as *Divine* perfection.

INSECURITY LOOP

—

It is a fact that there is money to be made from
our insecurities, and from our disempowerment.

We did not arrive here with any of these insecurities.
Capitalist, profit-hungry corporations have
diligently programmed us to buy into and
believe them at the subconscious level.

Over time, we have become stuck in that
insecurity loop that keeps us longing
for the stamp of approval on our lives.

The beauty of our being –
of our *human being,*
is the infinite, unique and imperfect
facets of humanity woven within us.

The true path lies in embracing
the beauty of our unique imperfection.
Through that embrace, we become empowered!

E-MOTION

—

We have all become great actors,
skilled at appearing as though we are okay.
We have been taught that '*positive*' emotions
are more socially acceptable than '*negative*' emotions.

There is no positive or negative
when it comes to emotions...
There is just energy in motion (e-motion).

Emotion is merely information that is signaling a greater
unmet need being communicated by our body and Soul.

Exploring our own darkness in order to heal is a
positive act of love... an act of self-love.
Being in our vulnerability and letting our emotions flow
naturally is what we ultimately want to strive for.

EMBRACING IMPERFECTION

–

Our conditioning within a system
of materialistic values,
has conned us to buy into
the unrealistic goal of perfection.
It has drawn us further away
from our natural guidance system,
which is driven intrinsically, from Soul level.

Perfection has no tangible value in our evolution.
The most beautiful and meaningful transformations are
at times messy, ugly, bizarre... and filled with mistakes,
imperfect action, and unexpected results along the way.

Rather than avoiding our imperfection,
let's instead seek out and embrace
the treasures hidden within it.

PATCHING CRACKS

—

The myth of perfection makes us
pathological in covering
up the cracks in our foundation.

Behind the façades we cover up with,
those cracks still exist…
preparing to open and crumble.

What if we accepted those so-called cracks?
Recognizing and acknowledging that those
cracks exist… that they are okay, and that
they do not make us any less than *who we are*.

On the contrary…
our cracks are part of
what makes us *who we are*.

COMPARISON

—

Comparison is embedded in us…
born of a societal-conditioned mindset,
rooted in the myth of perfection and scarcity.

Comparing ourselves to others, we may
feel our own shortcomings and insecurities.
Yet our natural state of being does not rest
on a binary of inferiority and superiority…
We simply are enough already.

What if we can adjust our perception
away from our comparisons, and instead
view it as an invitation into self-inquiry?

If we stop the comparison of ourselves to others
we naturally shift away from a scarcity mindset,
towards one grounded in a belief of infinite abundance.

Opening up to all that we already are and loving
ourselves unconditionally is always a work in progress...
An epic journey of unlearning and re-learning!

III

SOUL JOURNEY

RECLAIMING OUR POWER

—

Life is constantly offering us a choice:
to either move further away from
or closer to our empowerment.

It up to us to accept this invitation,
commit ourselves to a choice, and
then take consistent actions
aligned with that choice.

NUDGE

—

The question I ask
(myself) today is:
*"How do I want to
show up in this new world?"*

This is a rebuilding;
an emergence a new paradigm;
a shift in individual mindset
to propel a collective

T R A N S F O R M A T I O N .

THE COURAGE TO...

—

If we want to understand ourselves on a deeper level,
then we must cultivate the courage to do so.

The courage to be curious and to explore.
The courage to learn and to embrace change.

The courage to face and overcome our discomfort.
The courage to trust that we are *Divinely* supported.

The courage to tune out the external noise, and
the courage to be guided by the voice within.

DANCE OF LIFE

—

Life is truly an ongoing dance
of moving towards and away from
ourselves… and from each other.

All the experiences we have throughout our lives,
all of our *Dances,* are a part of who we are
in any given moment. They have shaped
who we are and how we show up.

Our *Dance* is our Soul's ongoing expression.

ENDINGS & BEGINNINGS

—

With every ending, we are offered a new beginning.

Life periodically presents us with sudden endings,
and these changes often lead us to question *Why?*

Frequently, these endings are actually
the gift of a brand-new beginning.
Initially, a new beginning may be rife
with trepidation and uncertainty because
we can't see what it holds fully (yet!).

UNIVERSE RISING

—

When it feels like the Universe
isn't working in your favour,
that's exactly what it is doing!

Be it a pause, a shake-up, or a loss…
sort through the contrast of life,
feel it, work through it,
and uncover the lesson(s).

Often we understand what is…
Because we know what isn't.

Trust that you are always Universally supported.
Whether a leap of faith, or letting go in surrender,
the Universe will rise to meet you.

SOUL INTEGRITY

–

We uphold the integrity of our Soul when
our actions are in alignment with our beliefs.

We are responsible for our *own* integrity.
We cannot be responsible for someone else's.

We are frequently presented
opportunties to embody our integrity...
to *BE* the embodiment of our integrity.

CHOICE

—

We can choose to move in ways that fulfill us
rather than those that keep us small or
perpetuate a false sense of security.

We can choose the way we want to love,
and to do the work that we want to do;
the love and the work that feeds our Soul.

We can empower ourselves through the choices
we make, or give away our power in victimhood.

Each moment offers us a choice.
What will you choose?

SELF-ABANDONMENT

–

Our socialization has normalized
self-abandonment across generations.

We have been conditioned
to view being selfish as negative,
and as a consequence of that message,
we may put ourselves and our needs last.

When life presents us with decisions to make,
we can ask ourselves this question:
Is this choice an act of self-love or self-abandonment?

SOUL JOURNEY

—

How can we be more intentional
with our individual evolution, so that
positive impacts ripple into the collective?

To continue evolving means to connect
deeper and deeper to the core of our being
with each turn on the spiral of life.

It means self-reflection, loosening ego's grip
and understanding we have work to do.
As we do that, we outgrow that old way of being,
shedding the layers of the stories
that we have armoured ourselves with;
other people's stories of who we are that
we have carried in order to feel seen and heard.

Feeling seen and heard as a false version of
ourselves is not truly being seen or heard at all.
We end up hurting ourselves and others,
even when the original intention
was protection and safety.

Getting to and connecting with the core of
our being, is a process of evolution.
It can be uncomfortable to stand in that truth
because people are used to us
the way we have historically shown up.
However, that wasn't really who we were;
and that isn't who we really are.

CREATIVE EXPRESSION

—

Our creative expression is
communication from our soul.
A key to our authentic wholeness,
to be all that we came here to be.

It is the key to unlock
the infinite love for ourselves;
the infinite love that is already;
the infinite love that we arrived here with.

We need only allow this expression so that we can
connect with and be in infinite love with others.

Creative expression is our Soul's desires,
messages, confirmations and light.
Creative expression is a portal via which
we connect with Universe, with our Soul.
Creativity is the *Divine Light* flowing through us,
and is meant to be shared generously.

HEALING IS A CHOICE

—

Often, we may become caught up in an inner struggle:
the choice between our desire to expand
versus our yearning for acceptance.

Our desire for change, be it healing or expansion,
is personal; a choice that comes from within us.

No one can force us to heal in order to expand;
nor can anyone else but us do our necessary inner work.

Others can support and encourage us,
yet we must possess a strong desire to
evolve in order to *allow* this healing journey.

WISDOM OF IMPERFECTION

–

Our imperfection is innate and *Divinely* designed.

It holds the waypoints of our Soul's journey.
Pit stops along the way to glean information;
to understand ourselves on a deeper level
and cultivate connection with our Soul.

Imperfection invites exploration and experimentation.

Embracing imperfection through
self-love and self-compassion is essential
as we travel a path of healing and evolving.
We discover that *we are enough, just as we are.*

UNCOMFORTABLE EVOLUTION

—

Healing is a requirement for our evolution.
Carrying around our unhealed wounds gets in the way
of our relationships: with others and with ourselves.

Becoming comfortable with being uncomfortable
is required if we want to heal, to grow or simply
try something new…if we want to change
specific parts of, or even all of our life.

Get comfortable with being uncomfortable.

EVOLVE OR REPEAT

—

Lessons in life will be repeated
until they are learned.

When confronted with life lessons,
we have two choices:
evolve or repeat.

We can quickly push the lesson away
to a hidden corner and seek
out ego-comforting distractions,
or we can pick it up
like a Rubik's cube
and explore the possibilities.

YOUR FUTURE SELF

—

Your future self is speaking to you…
waiting for you to listen;
to step into your power and embody
your greatest potential, now!

It is time to reclaim,
time to express…YOU!
Your essence,
your dreams,
your soul's desires,
your shining light,
your radiance…
your truth!

There is no time to waste and
no energy to be carelessly spent.
Haste not to get it ALL done now…
hasten to let go… in order to show up
in truth; bold, fierce, and awakened
to the power in your core being.

Surrender to the Divine plan:
believe in your worthiness,
open your arms and receive... it... ALL.

IV

SELF-EXPLORATION

IV

SELF-EXPLORATION

.

EXPANSION

—

Every moment is an opportunity for expansion.
Life is about learning, period.

We are not meant to stop gathering, reflecting,
questioning, and discovering new perspectives.

We are meant to stay curious,
just as we were as children.

This is our ongoing journey of expansion.

QUESTIONING

—

Why do we so frequently look
outside of ourselves for happiness?

Why was it never brought to our attention
as children to look inward for fulfillment?

Why do we all follow each other?
Why are we waiting for someone
to give us a check of approval?

Why do we agree to take
on beliefs that are not our own?

Why do we think failure is a negative thing?
Why is it often considered bad to ask questions?

Why do we ignore those nudges
and cries from our soul?

{R}EVOLUTION

—

Societal programming has us seeking external
validation and teaches us to fear failure.

We don't have to be afraid of failing;
failing is essential to our success.

It is inevitable and integral
to deepening our wisdom;
a precursor of true learning.

Our {R}evolution occurs in the
learning of how to trust our intuition,
our deep inner knowing,

We have all of the answers, and
everything we need within us, already.

We need only remember.

CURIOSITY

—

Our ability to expand and to grow
is inextricably linked to our curiosity.

Consider the nature of our curiosity
and also the curiosity of Nature.

Everything is connected,
and therein lies the curiosity.

PERSPECTIVE SHIFTS

—

It is okay to change your mind,
there is always time.

Even what you believed to be true
yesterday, last year or a moment ago.

The door is always open to step inside
and view life… to really see the
human experience from a new perspective.

A courageous, empowered choice to
shift your perspective individually,
will ripple out to benefit humanity.

OUR WOUNDS

—

The energy of our emotions attached
to our wounds and traumatic experiences
can remain with us our entire lives.

At the moment they happen,
we might not even comprehend
the full scope of their impact.

Often we downplay our pain.
Minimizing our trauma is
a survival mechanism.

Yet if we don't face the pain, and
instead bury it, that pain will resurface
in different forms throughout our lives.

Often our *wounds* are not our fault,
yet it is our responsibility to do the
inner work in order to heal them.

PATTERNS

—

Identifying our own behavioral
patterns offers us the opportunity
to choose differently the next time.

Many of us operate from a place of
unhealed wounds and pent-up emotions.
Built-up resentments become repeated
projection and mis-directed rage,
eventually becoming a default response.

That default will not change unless and
until awareness of our patterns enters in, and
we recognize that we can choose differently.

SELF-EXPLORATION

–

When we encounter radical life-changing moments,
or simply an internal urge to do something different,
it is happening so that we can reconfigure ourselves.

This is our moment to write a new chapter;
to continue walking the Universal spiral of life.

Resist the urge to slide into victimhood
when life suddenly shifts in a new direction.

Rather, accept the invitation into self-exploration,
embrace the opportunity with courage,
for it is the path back to yourself –
remembering who you came here to be.

DARKNESS

–

Do not be afraid of the darkness, or avoid it.

Instead, travel there with a good flashlight:
curiosity, gratitude, and the deep knowing
that you are just visiting briefly to learn.

In the process of seeking gratitude
for the simplicities of life,
is how we begin to see a
spark of light in the darkness.

HEALING

—

Healing is an ongoing process,
and it cannot be rushed.
Our Soul will offer us lessons, repeatedly…
until we finally learn them.

Begin by rejecting the societal conditioning
that we always need to be okay.
It is okay to not be okay.

Healing requires our humility, our courage,
and our vulnerability to be in our truth;
to be in our imperfections; and
to do better when we know better.

Understanding the truth that the work
our inner work, is never truly finished.
There is always more work to do, until
our Soul's evolution is complete.

FEELING

—

Healing is not logical or linear.
Healing is visceral. Healing is a spiral.
We do need to think our way through,
but more importantly we need
to feel our way through healing;
and that is the part that most people avoid.

True healing work takes us in all directions:
forward, sideways, upside down and sometimes
backwards… we may even find ourselves coming back
around for another perspective on an old wound.

Each layer is a deeper understanding.
There is always more to be uncovered,
and more to be processed and healed.
Facing it, feeling it, and honouring it.

We *feel* to understand our being, our Soul, and our Truth.
This is how we grow to love ourselves more, and
advance towards our wholesness being, in all areas
of our life… as our true authentic self.

OUR POTENTIAL

—

Our life experience is meant to bring that
which is implicit into the explicit.

We spend most of our experience trying to avoid
discomfort, along with parts of ourselves that
we don't understand, including our potential.

The parts of ourselves that we are tempted
to avoid aren't revealing a flaw,
they are revealing our humanity.

Ask yourself where you might be hiding
from the fullness of your potential.

ALWAYS MORE

—

There will often be moments
when we feel that we have
had a breakthrough or are
moving through life effortlessly.

Then out of nowhere, life reminds us
that this work is never finished.
There is always more to do.
There is always more of ourselves
to explore and cultivate a deeper connection.

This is one of the ways we can start
to re-write those old stories we have carried
that might have been clouded with
other people's visions of who we should be.

We get to decide who we are.
Our evolution is our choice.
We can write a new story for ourselves;
an exciting story of infinite expansion.

OUR TRUTH

—

When we start to show up differently
than other people are used to,
we may hear accusations and judgements:
'*You've changed!*' and '*Who do you think you are?*'

Everyone's ego thinks that they
know exactly who we are.
In fact, we are the only one
who can know our own truth.

Flipping the script, we can ask ourselves the question:
Who am I to step into the truth of who I am;
Who am I to step into my power?
The answer: *Well, who am I not to?*

ACCESSING OUR GIFTS

—

We each possess our own unique gifts.
For many of us, those gifts have remained
inaccessible and therefore untapped.

These gifts are only accessible when we
embody our true self; when our false layers
are peeled away; when we remember and
connect with the essence of who we truly are.

Our gifts are the expression of our unique essence.
Every moment can be an opportunity to step
into our truth, to remember that we are
all connected to one another.

Every moment can be an opportunity
to live and act and speak from
this space where our gifts are held, and
in so doing, we may continue to evolve.

COMFORT ZONE

—

In perpetually seeking our comfort zone we
are bypassing our growth opportunities:
spiritually, emotionally and physically.

Bypassing is hitting the *Easy Button* for life:
Escaping from pain with consumption of any kind,
and signaling to others that we are doing fantastic.
These are avoidance behaviours, a choice to feed
ego's comfort at the expense of Soul's growth.

Our deepest pleasures manifest through a lens
of exploration and learning, rather than one of escape.
Self-growth, becoming, and hearing Soul
is the true path of fulfillment in life.

V

EXPANSION

REMEMBERING WHO WE ARE

–

It is through our courage to show up for
the process of seeking and receiving
what is our divine inner wisdom
that we become our own greatest potential.

And then…we understand our purpose.

Lean into the discomfort of the lessons;
in order to remember who we are.

THE TIPPING POINT

—

Awareness arrives in this moment:

when the discomfort of staying stuck
outweighs the discomfort of taking
action to grow and to change.

How do you embrace your tipping points?

FEAR

–

Fear is only a feeling.
Fear will always be a part of our human experience,
No matter how evolved we have become.

Fear offers us some value in our
initial assessment of a new situation.

Our growth comes from having
an awareness of fear, and of
moving forward through it anyway.
This is our true courage.

We are not our fear.

SHINING LIGHTS

—

If we see someone shining
and sharing their gifts,
perhaps that might inspire us…

Rather than stir up envy or jealousy,
or feelings that something is owed to
us if we perhaps helped support it.

The true gift is in the witnessing
of the *Divine Light* shining.
That is what connects all of us.

No matter who is the one shining
their light at any given moment,
let it be a reminder that
we are all worthy of shining ours.

OUR INTENTIONAL JOURNEY

–

Our intentional journey of personal
exploration and expansion is not easy.

There are so many external forces
(people mostly, but ego too)
that would just as well have us stay stuck
where we are, expressly for their comfort.

Refuse and resist.
It can be uncomfortable for people
to experience us in our authenticity when
we have been hiding (parts of) it all along.

We may even hear phrases like *"you've changed."*
Yet, isn't that exactly the point when choosing an
intentional path of self-exploration and expansion?

DISCOMFORT-ABLE

—

Are you comfortable with being uncomfortable?
We have two choices: to evolve, or to repeat.

Discomfort is a fluid spectrum.
Oscillating between states of feeling stuck,
repeating what we don't want, and
the desire of choosing something different;
something more aligned with our path

Change occurs once the discomfort of one state
surpasses the discomfort of the other(s).
Once the pain of staying where we are right now,
outweighs the pain of choosing a new path,
and finally, we take action.

SHINE UNAPOLOGETICALLY

–

Recognize that not everyone is capable
of receiving you in your expansion.
Likely because they are still trapped
in a judgement & comparison paradigm.

That is about them!

Your responsibility is to your own well-being;
facing your truth head-on;
being empowered in shaping your life, in
harnessing the unlimited and unique creative
expression flowing through you.

That is your soul speaking!

Resist the urge to dim your light.
Shine, unapologetically!

TRANSMUTING PAIN

—

It's walking through, not around, the pain
that gifts us the most beautiful transformation.

There are many ways to process our feelings,
rather than to hide, to suppress, or to
continously seek to escape from them.

Choosing avoidance from negative feelings
is choosing short-term ego comfort
over long-term evolution of Soul.

Choosing avoidance is what keeps us stuck.
We transmute our pain by leaning into it.

Having compassion for ourselves as we brave
our way through our pain's depths is essential
in the unlearning and relearning of life.

So rather than judging and blaming
ourselves for feeling our emotions,
we can instead, give ourselves permission to feel
it all, reflect, release... and begin anew, transformed.

HIGHER SELF

—

Is there something that you are avoiding
that might be keeping you from
expanding into your Highest Self?

We miss opportunities when
we don't take appropriate risks.
We play it safe, we avoid pain
by letting our fear steer us.

We might stay in our self-limiting bubble
to mitigate the risk of potential discomfort
for showing up differently than others expect.

We avoid any discomfort and slowly, bit
by unconscious bit, our authenticity fades.
In avoiding discomfort, we slowly dim our
inner spark and we forget who we truly are.

To step outside our comfort, we risk: loss,
pain, failure, heartbreak and disappointment.
Yet, if we anchor in our comfort we risk not
fully experiencing life, love and our Higher Self.

Lean into to whatever it is that you might be avoiding,
and witness a path lighting up towards your Higher Self!

DEEPER MEANING

—

Every twist and turn, every person we meet,
every experience on our path, holds meaning.
They are coordinates on the map to our *Highest Self.*

Our squiggly path of experiences and people
are meant to teach us something (whether
we sought the learning, or not), to allow us to expand;
to enable us to better understand ourselves;
to mirror an internal feeling that needs processing;
or to simply be a soft landing-space in between.

The possibilities are infinite.
There is meaning in every connection,
whether it be for a moment, a season, or a lifetime.

STRETCH

—

Everything that we need to heal, to grow, to
expand and evolve, resides within us already.

It is up to us to seek it out,
explore, uncover and embrace it.

It is up to us to open ourselves to new
practices, new cultures, new perspectives,
and even new beliefs outside of our own.

This is our individual work of expansion.

Ultimately, our individual expansion benefits and
makes possible the expansion of the collective.

Stretch yourself by exploring something new, to
discover what works for you, what lights you up!

ALLOW

–

Whatever arises in any given moment in your
mental, physical and spiritual body... allow it.

Feel it all!
Feel it to heal it.

The negative experiences, the limiting beliefs,
and our spectrum of feelings are all
integral to our healing journey.

Allowing our emotions to flow is an act of self-love.
Through our emotions we can identify what
it is that we need in a given moment.

Feeling our emotions is retrieving data;
analyzing that data is how we come to understand.
Understanding what we need is how we know
what is required to bring resolve –
to learn, to grow, and to love ourselves.

REPURPOSED BRICKS

–

Here {inside}
You have built your HOME.

The foundation is strong:
each brick – a lesson,
each brick – reclaimed from the pile
of your self-limiting beliefs…
of your doubts, your fears,
your not-enoughness,
that for so many years have
covered up your *Divine* worth.

One by one, you have
repurposed those bricks…
into LOVE,
into TRUTH,
into SELF-WORTH
into BELIEF in yourself,
and this is your HOME.

EVOLUTION

—

As spiritual beings having a human
experience, we are meant to evolve.
We were never intended to be stagnant.
We are energy, and energy is in constant motion.

When we actively seek our evolution, through
our personal growth or a spiritual journey,
we are ultimately seeking to know ourselves;
to understand on a deeper level.

The challenge to that knowing arises because
our sense of identity often gets clouded
with the many competing narratives,
both internal & external; chosen or assigned:

"I am this," or *"I am that..."*
"Therefore I can't do this," or *"I can't do that."*

The solution to being present and conscious with
our evolution, lies in our unique creative expression.
Creativity is the direct connection with our Soul
that unlocks and fuels our evolution; our perpetual
motion forward into authentic wholeness of being.

SELF-LOVE PRACTICE

—

Self-love is not a destination,
but an ongoing practice.

We are always asking others what they
need or how they are doing (feeling), but is
it something we ask ourselves, regularly?

Can we extend that same love
and kindness to ourselves?

The areas within us that require attention
are constantly changing and evolving…
as is everything in the world around us.

Consider checking in with
yourself as a regular practice;
a daily commitment to self-care.

Ask yourself:
"Where do I need some extra LOVE today?"

This is self-compassion,
the root essence of self-love.

SCAFFOLDING

—

Failure is essential to our growth,
to our success and to our ultimate happiness.

Our societal belief systems have indoctrinated
us with the myth of perfection, programs
of shame and guilt, and that failure
is something to be avoided at all costs.

The truth is… failure is integral to our evolution.
We cannot truly grow in life without it.

Consider the possibility that failure often holds
our greatest lessons, and is the scaffolding
that helps us to reach our next level.

VI

UNCONDITIONAL LOVE

SOUL CALIBRATION

—

We are conditioned to look externally
for permission to do everything and anything;
for the nod to be ourselves; to not be too little
or too much for others... but just right.

We are attached to *Ego;* gripped by a need to be safe,
to be right, to be good, to be accepted and to be loved.
Ego is woven into everything we say and do…or don't.

Shaving off piece by piece, with these seemingly small
agreements, we slowly and unconsciously abandon ourselves;
we turn up the external chatter and disconnect from our Soul.
And in that gradual process, we forget *all that we are.*

Instead, what if we turned up our light?
What if we let the quiet voice inside of us speak?
Could this be where we remember *all that we are*?
Could this be where we reach our soul calibration?

SURRENDER

—

Sweet Soul, what is your desire?

What if you were to surrender?
Surrender to the uncomfortable & unknown.
Surrender control over outcome.
Surrender to the shadows of darkness.

Shine your light on that earthy, murky field.
Surrender to the light and guidance of the Universe.
There you will witness the lotus form.

Is it all you have ever dreamed of?
Yes, indeed. It is.

CORNERSTONE

—

The cornerstone of self-love is the belief
in our own inherent worthiness

Our healing journey brings us to a
deeper understanding of our worthiness.
Our belief in our worth will be tested.
In our healing, there are always more
dots to be revealed and connected.

Embodying courage through our choice,
loving ourselves every moment of our journey,
we can passionately embrace the beautiful
work-in-progress that we are!

OUR STORY

—

In our expansion,
we give ourselves
the permission to release
the burden of
other people's stories
about who we are…

and then we are free to just
BE… who WE ARE!

In simply being who we are
authentically and unapologeically,
we write our real and true story.

We can do so at any moment we choose.

SELF-WORTH

—

Life's endless experiences will attempt to
bring us back to questioning our worth.
[again and again]

Our societal conditioning is pervasive.
Nurturing our self-worth is our best defense.
Embodying belief in our self-worth is life altering!

Believing in, protecting, and nurturing
our self-worth is an ongoing investment... and a
revolutionary act of self-love that is never finished.

BOUNDARIES

—

Boundaries are part of the self-love equation.
If we say *Yes* when we really want to say *No*,
or vice-versa, we surrender our inner power.

Society has taught us to negotiate our worth,
trading pieces of ourselves and our natural
way of being in exchange for acceptance.

The ability to set healthy boundaries
is genuine emotional intelligence,
self-awareness and integrity of Soul.

Healthy boundaries give us agency over
our own energy and physical space.
They empower us to take charge of our
life, and to navigate it with resilience.

LOVE ME

–

It is important to remember
that our potential for love
– to love and be loved –
is only limited by the love
that we manifest for ourselves;
a love sourced from the inside out.

Love is so much more than
a description for a feeling...
Love is an activation.

When we love ourselves…
we embody love.
When we act through love,
by being authentic and true to self, it
ripples out into all of our relationships.

JUDGEMENT

—

Why are we constantly judging others?
By how they express themselves?
By their social media posts?
Or by anything at all?

In reality, the judgement of others
is ultimately judgement of ourselves.
We see parts of ourselves in one another.
We see our strengths, and our weaknesses
(and our insecurities).

Whatever the quality – whether inviting or
repulsive, and everything in between –
it exists in us, already.
That is why we can see it within another.

We never know what someone is truly
going through unless they speak it.
And so, let's not assume or judge,
one way or the other, or at all.

SELF-CARE

–

We are worthy of caring for and loving ourselves,
in the same way that we would want
others to care for and love us.

Invest time in the enjoyment of yourself.
Find meaning in developing a gratitude practice.
Self-care transports us to a
deeper intimacy with ourselves.

Direct some of your precious energy
inwards, as opposed to exclusively
outwards for others' benefit. This is how
we can experience the true joy of living.

In this way we build intimacy,
love and compassion for ourselves.
Through that connection to self,
we cultivate our capacity to share
deep love and compassion for others.

FORGIVENESS

—

A critical part of the healing
journey is forgiving yourself.

As you do the work of unravelling your old self,
recognize and accept that you did the best
that you could at each point in your life.

Have forgiveness for yourself!

Have forgiveness for the parts of yourself
that didn't feel fully worthy because
you let others write your story.

Have forgiveness for the choices that you
made, that kept you in the patterns of seeking
externally for love, acceptance and validation.

It is only through forgiveness that
your *Divine Light* can shine its brightest.

CREATING LOVE

—

Loving ourselves first is essential.
Loving ourselves first doesn't mean
that we don't love others around us.

When we love ourselves,
we believe in our inherent worthiness.
When we believe in our worthiness,
will live fuller, enriched lives of abundance.

Creating love for ourselves creates love for others.
Everybody benefits when we truly love ourselves.
Nurturing love and compassion within us
reverberates into all of our other relationships.

AS WE ARE

—

Unpacking the myth of perfection
is how we can begin to
embrace our imperfection
as innately intentional.

Imperfection reminds us that
nothing is in fact perfect.

Humanity itself was never intended to be.

Nature is also flawed and imperfect in its
beauty, and we are not separate from that.

Embracing imperfection allows
us to love ourselves as we already are.
We are liberated from the need to convince
anyone, including ourselves to love us.

In our authentic imperfection,
our wholeness of being can shine.

HUMILITY

—

Life is a spiral. Healing and growth is a spiral.
And the deeper it gets, the deeper it gets. We are never finished.

Through humility, we embody grace in knowing that we don't
have to have it all figured out, know it all, or always be right.

Through humility, we give ourselves permission to set ego
aside, and just be right where we are at any given moment.

Through humility we are open to beliefs,
perspectives and experiences different from our own.

Humility offers us a lens of navigating life here on Earth, in our
Divinely imperfect humanity, where we can all learn from each other.

Humility opens us to the possibility that we are ALL both the
teacher and the student having this human experience, together.

SYMBOL KEY

INFINITY SYMBOL (BEING)

Infinity is that which is boundless, endless, or larger than any natural number.
Our state of BE-ing is ongoing, infinite and therefore always to be continued.

CELTIC FIVE-FOLD (MYTHS)

The Celtic five-fold symbol represents the five elements, water, fire,
air, earth, and the spirit. The Soul's journey leads us to understand our Truth

TRISKELE (SOUL JOURNEY)

The Celtic Triskele, or Triple Spiral is the oldest symbol of spirituality, and
symbolizes an ancient Irish belief that everything happens in batches of 3.
It also represents the inner and outer worlds, the themes of birth, death,
and rebirth, as well as the unity of mental, physical, and spiritual self.

SYMBOL KEY

SPIRAL (SELF-EXPLORATION)

The spiral is an intuitive symbol of spiritual development and our identity with the Universe. The spiral symbolizes the journey inward, our healing and evolution. Our human journey is a spiral and we are constantly brought back to familiar themes to view life from new perspectives within our consciousness.

TREE OF LIFE (EXPANSION)

The tree of life is a symbol of longevity, wisdom, strength and our connection to a higher power. The tree of life is the connection between the earth and heaven; our expansion is a process of creating heaven here on Earth. The trunk symbolizes the masculine expression and the branches represent the feminine. As above, so below.

CELTIC TRINITY KNOT (UNCONDITIONAL LOVE)

The Celtic Trinity Knot (Triquetra) has no beginning and no end, representing eternity; The Celts believed anything of significance appeared in "threes," the Holy Trinity; mind, body and Spirit; or life, death and rebirth: the ongoing evolutionary journey of the Soul. Allowing the Soul's journey cultivates wholeness of being, of which the embodiment of unconditional self-love is the core essence.

ACKNOWLEDGEMENTS

T. M. CAMPBELL

—

Deepest gratitude to my two beautiful kids,
Jasmine Kaur Sikand and Deven Singh Sikand,
for choosing me to be your mama and to journey through this lifetime with.
Thank you for being my unconditional support system, for your wisdom,
for inspiring me daily to be a better human and to reach for my potential,
and for your encouragement to go after my dreams. We three. I love you.

Deep gratitude for my collaborator on this work and friend,
Robert T. Norton.
Thank you for the being the spark that ignited this work of creative
expression to be brought forth into the world and into the hands
of many. Here's to more collaborative and creative endeavors!

Deep gratitude for my soul family, especially these beautiful souls:
Carol Lynn Farr, Amy Bennett, Diane McClay and Nadine Searle, and
the many people from whom I have been gifted invaluable wisdom and
encouragement, and have made a meaningful impact during my soul's
journey and those who have allowed me to be a part of yours.

For YOU, the beautiful light reading this... for your courage to
continue to say YES to allowing your Soul's journey to unfold.
Here's to co-creating our infinite expansion!

ACKNOWLEDGEMENTS

ROBERT T. NORTON

—

I wish to offer massive gratitude to the following folks:

Stacey Persad for her generous encouragement, support, and friendship.

Sangdrub & Lochani for their Dharmic wisdoms and epic friendship.

Kathleen Lise Girard for making it all possible with her love and guidance!

I wish to offer especially extra massive gratitude to
my creative collaborator on this project:

T.M. Campbell

You inspire me with your courage, and your wisdom.
Please keep shining your Light!

ABOUT THE AUTHOR:

T. M. CAMPBELL

T.M. Campbell (Trish) is a Creatrix, Writer, Poet, Artist, Healing & Transformation Coach, Reiki Master Teacher, Podcast Host, and founder of INVIBE. Under the brand This is Trish, she is helping motivated individuals through the evolving, transformative process of healing and returning to self – to remember who they came here to be.

Reiki energy healing work became an integral part of that journey. As a writer, Trish is sharing her transformative journey with the world through written word to connect with and inspire others. Helping others through the profound path of healing has become Trish's life work.

WEBSITE:

thisistrishcampbell.com

OTHER TITLES:

LOVE ME: Awakening to Healing, Self-Love and Liberation

ISBN No. 978-1-77730519-2

LOVE ME Poetry: Self-Love and Soul Alchemy

ISBN No. 978-1-7387333-1-6

ABOUT THE AUTHOR:

ROBERT T. NORTON

The Greater Toronto Area (GTA) is the author's base camp for life, career,

the creative pursuits of photography, writing, painting and home renos,

as well as entrepreneurial pursuits in empowering education.

Love Me Meditations is his first collaborative writing project,

and it marks his fifth published book.

There will be more to follow, with two books already in progress.

WEBSITE:

soularts.studio

OTHER TITLES

Via Roma

ISBN No. 978-1-7753815-0-1

202122628427 – Full Moon Poems Whispered by a Muse

ISBN No. 978-1-7753815-2-5

Meditations in Photography Volume 1 – Connections to Creativity

ISBN No. 978-1-7753815-4-9

Meditations in Photography Volume 2 – Connections to Creativity

ISBN No. 978-1-7753815-6-3

Ingram Content Group UK Ltd.
Milton Keynes UK
UKHW010741150523
421757UK00001B/43